BAPTISM OF
DESIRE ~~

Also by Louise Erdrich

Novels

Love Medicine
The Beet Queen
Tracks

Poetry

Jacklight

BAPTISM OF
DESIRE ∽∽

poems

Louise Erdrich

HARPER & ROW, PUBLISHERS, New York
Grand Rapids, Philadelphia, St. Louis, San Francisco
London, Singapore, Sydney, Tokyo, Toronto

1817

FIRST EDITION

Designer: Cassandra J. Pappas

Library of Congress Cataloging-in-Publication Data

Erdrich, Louise.
    Baptism of desire : poems / Louise Erdrich.—1st ed.
      p. cm.
    ISBN 0-06-016213-9
    I. Title.
PS3555.R42B3   1989
811'.54—dc20   89–45650
                            Rev.

89 90 91 92 93 CC/RRD 10 9 8 7 6 5 4 3 2 1

For Michael
The flame and the source

Contents 〰

Part Three

Part Four

Part Five

Acknowledgments ~~~

The author thanks and acknowledges the editors of the various magazines in which some of these poems were published: *Caliban*—"Avila," "Orozco's Christ," "Angels"; *Granta*—"The Potchikoo Stories"; *Iowa Review*—"Translucence," "Sunflowers"; *Massachusetts Review*—"The Ritual"; *Northwest Review*—"The Sacraments"; *Paris Review*—"Birth," "The Fence"; *Partisan Review*—"Christ's Twin"; *Poetry*—"Fooling God"; *Prairie Schooner*—"The Flood," "The Return," "Bidwell Ghost."

Reconcile yourself to wait in this darkness as long as necessary, but still go on longing after him whom you love. For if you are to feel him or to see him in this life, it must always be in this cloud, in this darkness.

—*Anonymous fourteenth-century mystic,*
from The Cloud of Unknowing

I had grown much older during the last month—and my love, with all its excitements and sufferings, struck me as something very small and childish and trivial beside that other, unknown something which I could scarcely grasp and which frightened me like an unfamiliar, beautiful, but menacing face one tries in vain to make out in the gathering darkness.

—*Ivan Turgenev,*
"First Love"

PART ONE ～～

Fooling God ~~~

I must become small and hide where he cannot reach.
I must become dull and heavy as an iron pot.
I must be tireless as rust and bold as roots
growing through the locks on doors
and crumbling the cinderblocks
of the foundations of his everlasting throne.
I must be strange as pity so he'll believe me.
I must be terrible and brush my hair
so that he finds me attractive.
Perhaps if I invoke Clare, the patron saint of television.
Perhaps if I become the images
passing through the cells of a woman's brain.

I must become very large and block his sight.
I must be sharp and impetuous as knives.
I must insert myself into the bark of his apple trees,
and cleave the bones of his cows. I must be the marrow
that he drinks into his cloud-wet body.
I must be careful and laugh when he laughs.
I must turn down the covers and guide him in.
I must fashion his children out of playdough, blue, pink, green.
I must pull them from between my legs
and set them before the television.

I must hide my memory in a mustard grain
so that he'll search for it over time until time is gone.
I must lose myself in the world's regard and disparagement.
I must remain this person and be no trouble.

None at all. So he'll forget.
I'll collect dust out of reach,
a single dish from a set, a flower made of felt,
a tablet the wrong shape to choke on.

I must become essential and file everything
under my own system,
so we can lose him and his proofs and adherents.
I must be a doubter in a city of belief
that hails his signs (the great footprints
long as limousines, the rough print on the wall).
On the pavement where his house begins
fainting women kneel. I'm not among them
although they polish the brass tongues of his lions
with their own tongues
and taste the everlasting life.

Saint Clare ~✓~

She refused to marry when she was twelve and was so impressed by a Lenten sermon of Saint Francis in 1212 that she ran away from her home in Assisi, received her habit, and took the vow of absolute poverty. Since Francis did not yet have a convent for women, he placed her in the Benedictine convent near Basia, where she was joined by her younger sister, Agnes. Her father sent twelve armed men to bring Agnes back, but Clare's prayers rendered her so heavy they were unable to budge her.

—*John H. Delaney,*
Pocket Dictionary
of Saints

1 The Call

First I heard the voice throbbing across the river.
I saw the white phosphorescence of his robe.
As he stepped from the boat, as he walked
there spread from each footfall a black ripple,
from each widening ring a wave,
from the waves a sea that covered the moon.
So I was seized in total night
and I abandoned myself in his garment
like a fish in a net. The slip knots
tightened on me and I rolled
until the sudden cry hauled me out.
Then this new element, a furnace of mirrors,
in which I watch myself burn.
The scales of my old body melt away like coins,
for I was rich, once, and my father
had already chosen my husband.

2 *Before*

I kept my silver rings in a box of porphyrite.
I ate salt on bread. I could sew.
I could mend the petals of a rose.
My nipples were pink, my sister's brown.
In the fall we filled our wide skirts with walnuts
for our mother to crack with a wooden hammer.
She put the whorled meats into our mouths,
closed our lips with her finger
and said to Hush. So we slept
and woke to find our bodies arching into bloom.
It happened to me first,
the stain on the linen, the ceremonial
seal which was Eve's fault.
In the church at Assisi I prayed. I listened
to Brother Francis and I took his vow.
The embroidered decorations at my bodice
turned real, turned to butterflies and were dispersed.
The girdle of green silk, the gift from my father
slithered from me like a vine,
so I was something else that grew from air,
and I was light, the skeins of hair
that my mother had divided with a comb of ivory
were cut from my head and parceled to the nesting birds.

3 My Life As a Saint

I still have the nest, now empty,
woven of my hair, of the hollow grass,
and silken tassels at the ends of seeds.
From the window where I prayed,
I saw the house wrens gather
dark filaments from air
in the shuttles of their beaks.
Then the cup was made fast
to the body of the tree,
bound with the silver excresence of the spider,
and the eggs, four in number,
ale gold and trembling,
curved in a thimble of down.

The hinged beak sprang open, tongue erect,
screaming to be fed
before the rest of the hatchling emerged.
I did not eat. I smashed my bread to crumbs upon the sill
for the parents were weary as God is weary.
We have the least mercy on the one
who created us,
who introduced us to this hunger.

The smallest mouth starved and the mother
swept it out like rubbish with her wing.
I found it that dawn, after lauds,
already melting into the heat of the flagstone,
a transparent teaspoon of flesh,
the tiny beak shut, the eyes still sealed
within a membrane of the clearest blue.

I buried the chick in a box of leaves.
The rest grew fat and clamorous.
I put my hand through the thorns one night and felt the bowl,
the small brown begging bowl,
waiting to be filled.

By morning, the strands of the nest disappear
into each other, shaping
an emptiness within me that I make lovely
as the immature birds make the air
by defining the tunnels and the spirals
of the new sustenance. And then,
no longer hindered by the violence of their need,
they take to other trees, fling themselves
deep into the world.

4 Agnes

When you entered the church at Basia
holding the sceptor of the almond's
white branch, and when you struck
the bedrock floor, how was I to know
the prayer would be answered?
I heard the drum of hooves long in the distance,
and I held my forehead to the stone of the altar.
I asked for nothing. It is almost
impossible to ask for nothing.
I have spent my whole life trying.

I know you felt it, when his love spilled.
That ponderous light. From then on you endured
happiness, the barge you pulled
as I pull mine. This
is called density of purpose.
As you learned, you must shed everything else
in order to bear it.

That is why, toward the end of your life,
when at last there was nothing I could not relinquish,
I allowed you to spring forward without me.
Sister, I unchained myself. For I was always
the heaviest passenger,
the stone wagon of example,
the freight you dragged all the way to heaven,
and how were you to release yourself
from me, then, poor mad horse,
except by reaching the gate?

Avila 〜🙰〜

Teresa of Avila's brother, Rodrigo, emigrated to America in 1535 and
died in a fight with Natives on the banks of the Rio de la Plata.

—*footnote to* The Life of Teresa of Jesus,
translated and edited by E. Allison Peers

Sister, do you remember our cave of stones,
how we entered from the white heat of afternoons,
chewed seeds, and plotted one martyrdom
more cruel than the last?
You threw your brown hair back
and sang Pax Vobiscum to the imaginary guard,
a leopard on the barge of Ignatius.
Now I see you walking toward me, discalced like the poor,
as the dogwood trees come into blossom.
Their centers are the wounds of nails,
deep and ragged. The spears of heaven
bristle along the path you take,
turning me aside.

Dear sister, as the mountain grows out of the air,
as the well of fresh water
is sunk in the grinding sea,
as the castle within rises stone upon stone,
I still love you. But that is only
the love of a brother for a sister, after all,
and God has nothing to do with it.

Immaculate Conception ~~

for Eileen Cowin

It was not love. No flowers or ripened figs
were in his hands, no words
in his mouth. There was no body
to obstruct us from each other.
The sun was white-hot, a brand
that sank through me and left no mark.
Yet I knew. And Joseph,
poor Joseph with his thick palms,
wearing antlers.
What could he do but wash
the scorched smell from the linen?
What could he do but fit the blades
of wood together into a cradle?

The rain fell and the leaves closed
over us like a shield.
A small light formed and the taper
that held it aloft
was dipped many times into my blood.
Now the being rests in the bowl of my hips.
There is no turning. Already
the nails are forged.
The tree thickens.

The Savior ~✒~

When the rain began to fall, he rolled back
into the clouds and slept again.
Still it persisted, beating at every surface,
until it entered his body
as the sound of prolonged
human weeping.

So he was broken.
His first tears dissolved
the mask of white stone.
As they traveled through the bones of his arms,
his strength became a mortal strength
subject to love.

On earth, when he heard the first rain
tap through the olive leaves,
he opened his eyes and stared at his mother.
As his father, who had made the sacrifice,
stood motionless in heaven,
his son cried out to him:

I want no shelter, I deny
the whole configuration.
I hate the weight of earth.
I hate the sound of water.
Ash to ash, you say, but I know different.
I will not stop burning.

C h r i s t ' s   T w i n ~~~

He was formed of chicken blood and lightning.
He was what fell out when the jug tipped.
He was waiting at the bottom
of the cliff when the swine plunged over.
He tore out their lungs with a sound like ripping silk.
He hacked the pink carcasses apart, so that the ribs spread
like a terrible butterfly, and there was darkness.
It was he who turned the handle and let the dogs
rush from the basements. He shoved the crust
of the volcano into his roaring mouth.
He showed one empty hand. The other gripped
a crowbar, a monkey wrench, a crop
which was the tail of the ass that bore them to Egypt,
one in each saddlebag, sucking twists
of honeyed goatskin, arguing
already over a woman's breasts.
He understood the prayers that rose
in every language, for he had split the human tongue.
He was not the Devil nor among the Fallen—
it was just that he was clumsy, and curious,
and liked to play with knives. He was the dove
hypnotized by boredom and betrayed by light.
He was the pearl in the mouth, the tangible
emptiness that saints seek at the center of their prayers.
He leaped into a shadow when the massive stone
rolled across the entrance, sealing him with his brother
in the dark as in the beginning.

Only this time he emerged first, bearing the self-
inflicted wound, both brass halos
tacked to the back of his skull.
He raised two crooked fingers; the extra die
tumbled from his lips when he preached
but no one noticed. They were too busy
clawing at the hem of his robe and planning
how to sell him to the world.
They were too busy drinking
at the fountain.
They were drunk.
They would drown for love.

Orozco's Christ ~✌~

Who rips his own flesh down the seams and steps
forth flourishing the axe,
who chops down his own cross,
who straddles it,
who stares like a cat,
whose cheeks are the gouged blue of science,
whose torso springs out of wrung cloth
blazing ochre, blazing rust, whose blood
cools to black marble in his fist,
who makes his father kneel,
who makes his father say,
"You want her? Take her."
Who rolls the stone from the entrance over his mother,
who pulls her veil out from under it,
who ties the stained cloth around his hips
and starts out,
walking toward Damascus, toward Beirut,
where they are gathering in his name.

Mary Magdalene 〜〜

I wash your ankles
with my tears. Unhem
my sweep of hair
and burnish the arch of your foot.
Still your voice cracks
above me.

I cut off my hair and toss it across your pillow.
A dark towel
like the one after sex.
I'm walking out,
my face a dustpan,
my body stiff as a new broom.

I will drive boys
to smash empty bottles on their brows.
I will pull them right out of their skins.
It is the old way that girls
get even with their fathers—
by wrecking their bodies on other men.

Angels ~~~

The cats wind together in the barn.
Their weightless bodies fly across the field like scarves.
Draped on a woodpile, vibrating
in a patch of sun,
their eyes are frozen glass.
Their mouths,
lined with rose petals,
shirred with bloody silks
and bone needles,
open with the delicate interest
of the very old angels, the first ones,
in whose eyes burned the great showers of the damned.

The Sacraments ⌒∫⌒

Baptism, Communion, Confirmation,
Matrimony, Holy Orders, Extreme Unction

1

As the sun dancers, in their helmets of sage,
stopped at the sun's apogee
and stood in the waterless light,
so, after loss, it came to this:
that for each year the being was destroyed,
I was to sacrifice a piece of my flesh.
The keen knife hovered
and the skin flicked in the bowl.
Then the sun, the life that consumes us,
burst into agony.

We began, the wands and the bracelets of sage,
the feathers cocked over our ears.
When the bird joined the circle and called,
we cried back, shrill breath,
through the bones in our teeth.
Her wings closed over us, her dark red
claws drew us upward by the scars,
so that we hung by the flesh,

as in the moment before birth
when the spirit is quenched
in whole pain, suspended
until there is no choice, the body
slams to earth,
the new life starts.

2

It is spring. The tiny frogs pull
their strange new bodies out
of the suckholes, the sediment of rust,
and float upward, each in a silver bubble
that breaks on the water's surface,
to one clear unceasing note of need.

Sometimes, when I hear them,
I leave our bed and stumble
among the white shafts of weeds
to the edge of the pond.
I sink to the throat,
and witness the ravenous trill
of the body transformed at last and then consumed
in a rush of music.

Sing to me, sing to me.
I have never been so cold
rising out of sleep.

3

I was twelve, in my body
three eggs were already marked
for the future.
Two golden, one dark.
And the man,
he was selected from other men,
by a blow on the cheek
similar to mine.
That is how we knew,
from the first meeting.
There was no question.
There was the wound.

4

It was frightening, the trees in their rigid postures
using up the sun,
as the earth tilted its essential degree.
Snow covered everything. Its confusing glare
doubled the view
so that I saw you approach
my empty house
not as one man, but as a landscape
repeating along the walls of every room
papering over the cracked grief.

I knew as I stepped into the design,
as I joined the chain of hands,
and let the steeple of fire
be raised above our heads.
We had chosen the costliest pattern,
the strangest, the most enduring.
We were afraid as we stood between the willows,
as we shaped the standard words with our tongues.
Then it was done. The scenery multiplied
around us and we turned.
We stared calmly from the pictures.

5

God, I was not meant to be the isolate
cry in this body.
I was meant to have your tongue in my mouth.

That is why I stand by your great plaster lips
waiting for your voice to unfold from its dark slot.

Your hand clenched in the shape of a bottle.
Your mouth painted shut on the answer.
Your eyes, two blue mirrors, in which I am perfectly denied.

I open my mouth and I speak
though it is only a thin sound, a leaf
scraping on a leaf.

6

When the blue steam stalls over the land
and the resinous apples
turn to mash, then to a cider whose thin
twang shrivels the tongue,
the snakes hatch
twirling from the egg.

In the shattered teacup, from the silvering
boards of the barn,
in the heat of rotting mulch hay,
they soak up the particles of light

so that all winter
welded in the iron sheath
of sludge under the pond
they continue, as we do,
drawing closer to the source,
their hearts beating slower
as the days narrow
until there is this one pale aperture
and the tail sliding through

then the systole, the blackness of heaven.

PART TWO ~~

Rudy Comes Back ～⌇～

I knew at once, when the lights dimmed.
He was pissing on the works.
The generator fouled a beat
and recovered.
My doors were locked
anyway, and the big white dog
unchained in the yard.

Outside, the wall of hollyhocks
raved for mercy from the wind's strap.
The valves of the roses opened,
so sheltering his step
with their frayed mouths.

I don't know how he entered
the dull bitch at my feet.
She rose in a nightmare's hackles,
glittering, shedding heat
from her mild eyes.

All night we kept watch,
never leaving the white-blue ring
of the kitchen. I could hear him out there,
scratching in the porch hall, cold
and furtive as a cat in winter.
Toward dawn I got the gun.

And he was there, Rudy J.V. Jacklitch,
the bachelor who drove his light truck
through the side of a barn on my account.
He'd lost flesh. The gray skin of his face dragged.
His clothes were bunched.

He stood reproachful,
in one hand the wooden board,
and the pegs, still my crib.
In the other the ruined bouquet
of larkspur I wouldn't take.

I was calm. This was something I'd forseen.
After all, he took my name down to hell,
a thin black coin.
Repeatedly, repeatedly, to his destruction,
he called.
And I had not answered then.
And I would not answer now.

The flowers chafed to flames of dust in his hands.
The earth drew the wind in like breath and held on.
But I did not speak
or cry out
until the dawn, until the confounding light.

Mary Kröger ~~~

1

Sometimes I had such fury I would choose
the knife and hone it keen, I thought his heart
was small and dark, a whetstone for my tooth.
I thought his eyes had character at first,
but that was just exhaustion, schnapps, the truth
is that I left him in my sleep,
traveling through the whiteness where he could not follow,
descending through the lovely danger,
to where the waves boomed and hissed.
Those dreams were nothing. I had barrels
to unload each morning. I had salt
to plunge my hands in till they shrank.
I talked to him, let hot words bloom and smoke
like ashen flowers fragile in the sheets.
Beneath his hand I faltered and my rage
was managed for me, blown to particles
that came together again and hardened
in the slow, unfiltered afternoons.

2

I had my nerve, my shackles, and those dreams
that killed me with their vehemence, and him,
who lit red votive candles for my womb,
but I was barren that way, it's just one
way to be empty, Otto, one,
and I've a thriving scheming mind
that's good with numbers.
He did not relent,
so hounded past all sense,
I threw the twenty-dollar roasts to dogs.
A wasted animal, my anger healed
all wrong. It walked on elbows,
ate and screamed,
until there was no living with it.

God, who in your pity made a child
to slaughter on a tree, why don't you just
fix the damn thing and be done with it?
I prayed. That year the mayflies came
or angels, take your pick, in haste to crush
themselves together in a cloudy paste
and clog our engine parts.

There's luck, there's luck, I've seen luck pass and fall
on less deserving strangers. There's poor Clare
who bore her child then threw it down a well.
The sorry fool. She had a creed, a name,
a hand to look for in a cloud,
a purpose in a fast distilling life
that comes to this—a stone, a knife,
ten years, and the slow patience of steel.

Poor Clare 〜〰〜

April was the thickest month for birth.
We noticed, counting back, the county fair
held nine months ago on low grounds by the river,
a flattened oxbow plain surrounded by elms.
The great smashed tree limbs littered all around
and brush grown through to cover every sin
beyond the stockbarns there, made breeding pens
where Clare went following the carnie men.

A soft girl, heavy in the hips, with weak
blue lashless eyes and curdled cream for skin,
she altered herself to each occasion.
She wasn't bad, just dull, and much too eager
for a man's touch as she had no father.
At night, her mother nailed the door,
but Clare hid rope and swung down from the eaves
and met men there, so some of us believe

because each night as long as the fair went on
she rode wild on the ferris wheel, the cups,
the roundelet, the bullet, octopus
and dressed in pink, orange feathers won at dice
till there could hardly be a speck of doubt
at how she paid, among the twisted branches
where the wild grass spread too long and in the winter
flattened like hair under tons of snow.

Clare's mother was a hard one, shrewd and big
with iron wadding in the bears she stuffed
and sold in the seamstress shop
she ran from her glassed-in porch.
Poor Clare, she sewed a pup tent, wore it out,
and in the last month everybody talked,
then she deflated slowly so by summer
there was no sign and no sign of the child either.

And never has been, so the town appears
different to me and the secret holds.
Each street's a hiding place with bushes, sewers,
trash dumps, drainpipes, hollow stumps and rocks.
The mother's mute and stuffs her toys in rage.
The cops and social workers fill out reams
of forms in triplicate and single space.
Poor Clare blinks her beaded lashes and defies
each document in silence. Her child is ashes,

carried downriver, laid in a manger, rooted,
dry as grain in a long straight windbreak,
blooming white year after year.
And there's no help to it but I have dreamed
I followed her to the great uprooted wrecks
and there in the massive spirals of dirt-dead roots,
saved the child and buried Clare instead, so now,
when the river comes, flooding the whole park,
the child stumbles toward me on silver feet.

I've risen, I've gone out, I've searched
the yard, the scalding tubs, the massed black thorns.
I've heard its high thin bawl and crept
along the split foundation of our house,
whining to it like a dog or an anxious ewe,
till I woke and feared my mind was bent.
And nobody, and the cry still faint
as air through a sieve.

B i d w e l l   G h o s t ～〆～

Each night she waits by the road
in a thin white dress
embroidered with fire.

It has been twenty years
since her house surged and burst in the dark trees.
Still nobody goes there.

The heat charred the branches
of the apple trees,
but nothing can kill that wood.

She will climb into your car
but not say where she is going
and you shouldn't ask.

Nor should you try to comb the blackened nest of hair
or press the agates of tears
back into her eyes.

First the orchard bowed low and complained
of the unpicked fruit,
then the branches cracked apart and fell.

The windfalls sweetened to wine
beneath the ruined arms and snow.
Each spring now, in the grass, buds form on the tattered wood.

The child, the child, why is she so persistent
in her need? Is it so terrible
to be alone when the cold white blossoms
come to life and burn?

The Kitchen Gods ~~

When my husband is sleeping,
they step from the wall,
mincing over the cold burners
on their hook feet,
keeping balance
with umbrellas of soot.
Where do they go to consort?
The night is blue.
The willows on my teacups
bend above a bridge.
I hear them now, kissing,
their fragile lips clink.
They are chipping
at one another,
cups in raw water,
scratching their blood-red lacquers
until the plaster
shows white and the wires appear.
I painted the man's belled coat,
the woman's skirt, deep red.
Now they vanish among the branches in the teacups,
the whips and rings.
I know there will be no rest for me.
No thimbleful of peace.

The Carmelites ~~~

They're women, not like me but like the sun
burning cold on a winter afternoon,
audacious brilliance from a severe height,
living in the center as the town revolves
around them in a mess. Of course
we want to know what gives behind their fence,
behind the shades, the yellow brick
convent huge in the black green pines.
We pass it, every one of us, on rounds
we make our living at. There's one
I've spoken to. Tall, gaunt, and dressed in brown,
her office is to fetch the mail, pay bills,
and fasten wheat into the Virgin's arms.
I've thought of her, so ordinary, rising every night,
scarred like the moon in her observance,
shaved and bound and bandaged
in rough blankets like a poor mare's carcass,
muttering for courage at the very hour
cups crack in the cupboards downstairs, and Otto
turns to me with urgency and power.
Tremendous love, the cry stuffed back, the statue
smothered in its virtue till the glass corrodes,
and the buried structure shows,
the hoops, the wires, the blackened arcs,
freeze to acid in the strange heart.

PART THREE ~~

H y d r a ~~~

1

Blessed one, beating your tail across heaven,
uncoiling through the length of my life,
each bone of the spine a measure, a day,
each diamond, each trillium star.

The hinged mouth swings wide at birth, the dark
peristalsis, the great swallowing begins.
The child's first lesson is the iron knocker,
the hasp of hunger opening.

I saw gasoline leaking from the corners of a woman's eyes,
her hands among the crushed stalks,
searching for the hands of her children,
as the grain was put to fire.

I saw a girl's life drawn through the ring
as a magician pulls linked scarves
from the mouth of a child, the colors
bright and primary as the inside of the body.

The boat, rocking at the quarter moon.
The innocent, recovered in a sling of holes.
The drowned, pumped and jacketed.
The dead, waking to the wild, dark laughter.

I stayed inside the body of my mother
as long as possible, I welded
my body to the lean arc of my father,
the skater, as together

on the ice we scratched the sign of eternity,
the figure eight, until the white grooves matched,
the blades dulled, our knees
locked and trembled.

Hour of the talk-show hostess.
Hour of the wolf, of the tree service,
of the worship of the god whose name adds
to a single year. Abraxas, the perfect word.

2

Christmas, the angel strikes the earth
with his caduceus. Snakes fly from the rocks.
The scrolls are unsealed and the taxes
are levied in gold, in Nazareth.

The child is delivered in its garment
of wax, and his mother's blood
darkens the straw. The oxen kneel,
as they would otherwise, in sleep, and the low note
begins, the note of hunger, by which He learns
what it is to be degraded, to be human,
as the cold star rises to its azimuth
showing the path.

In the New Year the snake shifts its coils,
arranging the dark profusion.
God's subtle machinery grinds the moon's silvers,
and the old is shed, the husk of black paper.

Now we can walk in the longer spears of light,
as the scales give back our faces,
magnified, glowing with the promise of the resurrection.
Again, the child is whipped toward the place of skulls.

Again, the slashed wools, the carcass
of the lamb flung on the altar,
and the cone of fire wraps and consumes
the sacrifice in spring.

I do not want to sleep.
I do not want to be fed through the lips.
I do not want the harrow of need to pass over my body.
I do not want my children to crave me.

Lies, lies!
I stand in my gilded harness,
my halo of bees.
I stand in the gold dust of sex

giving birth to the last of our children,
the dark red stone.
Peridot.
Eye of the bronze serpent.

3

Binding of old dazzlement,
laces of uncured hide,
I take from my mouth the stopper of felt.
I pull you out by the tail.

I release myself cell by cell,
from the pieties, the small town
monks of platitudes, the crystal of Christ Tortured
sold on Shoppers Cable Network.

I unlink the scarves, I smash
the gold-filled chain, the bracelet
of tiny commemorative charms,
the ski-boot, the pom-pom, the silver typewriter.

I tear the hook from my mouth.
I bleed from the lips, the gapped
flesh. I take up the carving knife,
and swim for the Captain of the Launch.

4

Here we are in the sacred monotony.
Here we are riding the snake,
stuck on each radiant spine, as the days
shorten toward the equinox.

In the gravel bed-blankets,
we are scratching a darker hole
to the core where we will sleep
now, as the earth heals over

all traces of our passage.
No dropped spoon, nothing left behind.
No woman to guide us back into her body
the same way we left.

Snake uncoiling from the bound
woman's arms, from the throat
like a necklace of shorn flesh, like nerves
laced into a fretwork of awareness.

Consciousness, the decorative experiment,
feeding on every other species.
Hydra, multifarious source
of harm. Lucent, ineradicable.

Serpent of the mouth clasped to tail,
of the benzene vision. Serpent of the half gender,
longing to join its opposite, in tenderness
to perfect the old brutalized animal.

As you stood before me, your palms
to the first sun, incised with my name.
As you walked from the woods fully formed.
As you came down from the mountain with my son.

As we rocked ourselves to sleep, as we woke
in the hushed bank of reeds,
to the storm moving in, a cave of gold lightning,
first moon like the handle on a jug of wine.

If I descended into the basement of my Polish grandmother,
unsealed the whole chickens canned in jars.
If they emerged, virginally outraged,
drying their rough new feathers . . .

If I went back to Wahpeton, North Dakota,
on All Soul's Night, if I returned to each house
and embraced the high school band leader
and the telemarketer, flung on the moon-dark couch . . .

If I finally learned to crochet
and began the world's longest scarf,
my need to perfect myself, my legacy.
If I died at the needles . . .

5

The world tips away in plenary motion,
as our daughters ascend the basement stairs.
They dance toward us in their sequined crowns
waving their wands of paste and glitter.

Even now, the pages are bound and sewn,
the yellow sticks counted and dispersed.
I watch the women pass
with their jars of rose-oil, of pink ammonia.

Snake of the heat-seeking venom,
of the flask of rage,
the long wait in the sun.
Snake of the double helix, the orange rind.

Snake of the long reach, the margin,
the perfect sideways motion
I have imitated all my life.
Snake of hard hours, you are my poetry.

According to God, your place is low,
under Adam's heel, but as for me,
a woman shaped from a secondary bone,
who cares if you wrap my shoulders?
Who cares if you whisper? Who cares
if the fruit is luscious? Your place
is at my ear.

Notes

"Hydra" and most of the other poems in this book were written between the hours of two and four in the morning, a period of insomnia brought on by pregnancy.

Hydra was the nine-headed serpent slain by Hercules in the marsh of Lerna. Each head when cut off was succeeded by two new ones, unless the wound was cauterized. Hydra is also a multifarious source of destruction that cannot be eradicated by any single attempt, and it is the southern constellation below Cancer, also called the Water Monster.

According to the second edition of *Webster's New International and Unabridged Dictionary, abraxas* is a name containing Greek letters which as numerals amount to 365. It is, therefore, a mystical word, a charm engraved on gemstones, and a god of uncertain origin worshiped by Gnostics and various Christian Gnostic sects from the second century. The Egyptian Basilides regarded him as the Supreme Deity, the source of mind and word. As a form of sun god, he is represented with the head of a cock or lion, a human body, and serpents as legs.

The German biochemist August Kekule von Stradonitz envisioned the ring structure of benzene with the help of a dream in which he saw a snake swallowing its tail.

In *The Dreaming Brain* (Basic Books, 1988), J. Allan Hobson investigates the sleeping brain. "We know that the internal communication from nerve cell to nerve cell is a continuous process: night and day it goes on and on and on. And we know that this ongoing nervous activity is spontaneous: it changes in relation to signals from the external world, coding them in its own way into its own language. But it is not created by—nor is it dependent upon—external inputs. And we know that during sleep the ratio of external to internal signaling changes; during dreaming sleep there is just as much activity going on within the system as there is during working. In other words, during dreams the system is literally talking to itself."

And, finally, from "Concerning the Serpent," one of the pieces in "The Acts of Thomas" section of *The Other Bible* (ed. Willis Barnstone, Harper & Row, 1984): Judas Thomas, the Twin of the Messiah, met a great serpent during his wanderings in India and questioned him, saying: "Tell me of what seed and what race you are."

> And he [the serpent] said to him: "I am a reptile of reptile nature, the baleful son of a baleful father; I am son of him who hurt and smote the four standing brothers. . . . I am kins man of him who is outside the ocean, whose tail is set in his own mouth; I am he who entered through the fence into Paradise and said to Eve all the things that my father charged me to say to her.

PART FOUR ～～

Potchikoo's Life After Death ~~~

How They Don't Let Potchikoo into Heaven

After Old Man Potchikoo died, the people had a funeral for his poor crushed body, and everyone felt sorry for the things they had said while he was alive. Josette went home and set some bread by the door for him to take on his journey to the next world. Then she began to can a bucket of plums she'd bought cheap, because they were overripe.

As she canned, she thought how it was. Now she'd have to give away these sweet plums since they had been her husband's favorites. She didn't like plums. Her tastes ran sour. Everything about her did. As she worked, she cried vinegar tears into the jars before she sealed them. People would later remark on her ingenuity. No one else on the reservation pickled plums.

Now, as night fell, Potchikoo got out of his body, and climbed up through the dirt. He took the frybread Josette had left in a towel, his provisions. He looked in the window, saw she was sleeping alone, and he was satisfied. Of course, since he could never hold himself back, he immediately ate the bread as he walked the long road, a mistake. Two days later, he was terribly hungry, and there was no end in sight. He came to the huge luscious berry he knew he shouldn't eat if he wanted to enter the heaven all the priests and nuns described. He took a little bite, and told himself he'd not touch the rest. But it tasted so good tears came to his eyes. It took a minute, hardly that, for him to stuff the whole berry by handfuls into his mouth.

He didn't know what would happen now, but the road was still there. He kept walking, but he'd become so fat from his greed that when he came to the log bridge, a test for good souls, he couldn't balance to cross it, fell in repeatedly, and went on cold and shivering. But he was dry again, and warmer, by the time he reached the pearly gates.

Saint Peter was standing there, dressed in a long, brown robe, just as the nuns and priests had always said he would be. He examined Potchikoo back and front for berry stains, but they had luckily washed away when Potchikoo fell off the bridge.

"What's your name?" Saint Peter asked.

Potchikoo told him, and then Saint Peter pulled a huge book out from under his robe. As the saint's finger traveled down the lists, Potchikoo became frightened to think how many awful deeds would be recorded after his name. But as it happened, there was only one word there. The word *Indian*.

"Ah," Saint Peter said. "You'll have to keep walking."

Where Potchikoo Goes Next

So he kept on. As he walked, the road, which had been nicely paved and lit when it got near heaven, narrowed and dipped. Soon it was only gravel, then dirt, then mud, then just a path beaten in the grass. The land around it got poor too, dry and rocky. And when Potchikoo got to the entrance of the Indian heaven, it was no gate of pearl, just a simple pasture gate of weathered wood. There was no one standing there to guard it, either, so he went right in.

On the other side of the gate there were no tracks, so Potchikoo walked aimlessly. All along the way, there were chokecherry bushes, not quite ripe. But Potchikoo was so hungry again that he raked them off the stems by the handful and gobbled them down, not even spitting out the pits.

The dreadful stomachaches he got, very soon, were worse than hunger, and every few steps poor Potchikoo had to relieve himself.

On and on he went, day after day, eating berries to keep his strength up and staggering from the pain and shitting until he felt so weak and famished that he had to sit down. Some time went by, and then people came to sit around him. They got to talking. Someone built a fire, and soon they were roasting venison.

The taste of it made Potchikoo lonesome. Josette always fried her meat with onions.

"Well," he said, standing up when he was full, "it's time to go now."

The people didn't say good-bye though—they just laughed. There were no markers in this land, nothing but extreme and gentle emptiness. It was made to be confusing. There were no landmarks, no lookouts. The wind was strong, and the bushes grew quickly, so that every path made was instantly obscured.

But not Potchikoo's path. At regular intervals new chokecherry bushes had sprung up from the seeds that had passed through his body. So he had no trouble finding his way to the gate, out through it, and back on the road.

Potchikoo's Detour

Along the way back, he got curious and wondered what the hell for white people was like.

As he passed the pearly gates, Saint Peter was busy checking in a busload of Mormons, and so he didn't even look up and see Potchikoo take the dark fork in the road.

Walking along, Potchikoo began to think twice about what he was doing. The air felt warm and humid, and he expected it to get worse, much worse. Soon the screams of the damned would ring out and the sky would turn pitch-black. But his curiosity was, as always, stronger than his fear. He kept walking until he came to what looked like a giant warehouse.

It was a warehouse, and it was hell.

There was a little sign above the metal door marked ENTRANCE, HELL. Potchikoo got a thrill of terror in his stomach. He carefully laid his ear against the door, expecting his blood to curdle. But all he heard was the sound of rustling pages. And so, gathering his courage, he bent to the keyhole and looked in to see what it was the white race suffered.

He started back, shook his head, then bent to the keyhole again.

It was worse than flames.

They were all chained, hand and foot and even by the neck, to old Sears Roebuck catalogues. Around and around the huge warehouse they dragged the heavy paper books, mumbling, collapsing from time to time to flip through the pages. Each person was bound to five or six, bent low beneath the weight. Potchikoo had always wondered where old Sears catalogues went, and now he knew the devil gathered them, that they were instruments of torment.

The words of the damned, thin and drained, rang in his ears all the way home.

Look at that wall unit. What about this here recliner? We could put up that home gym in the basement.

Potchikoo Greets Josette

On his journey through heaven and hell, Potchikoo had been a long time without sex. It was night when he finally got back home, and he could hardly wait to hold Josette in his arms. Therefore, after he had entered the house and crept up to her bed, the first words he uttered to his wife in greeting were "Let's pitch whoopee."

Josette yelled and grabbed the swatter she kept next to her bed to kill mosquitoes in the dark. She began to lambast Potchikoo until she realized who it was, and that this was no awful dream.

Then they lay down in bed and had no more thoughts.

Afterward, lying there happily, Potchikoo was surprised to find that he was still passionate. They began to make love again, and still again, and over and over. At first Josette returned as good as Potchikoo gave her, but after a while it seemed that the more he made love, the more need he felt and the more heat he gave off. He was unquenchable fire.

Finally, Josette fell asleep, and let him go on and on. He was so glad to be alive again that he could never remember, afterward, how many times he had sex that night. Even he lost count. But when he woke up late the next day, Potchikoo felt a little strange, as though there was something missing. And sure enough, there was.

When Potchikoo looked under the covers, he found that his favorite part of himself was charred black, and thin as a burnt twig.

Potchikoo Restored

It was terrible to have burnt his pride and joy down to nothing. It was terrible to have to face the world, especially Josette, without it. Potchikoo put his pants on and sat in the shade to think. But not until Josette left for daily Mass and he was alone, did Potchikoo have a good idea.

He went inside and found a block of the paraffin wax that Josette used to seal her jars of plum pickles. He stirred the coals in Josette's stove and melted the wax in an old coffee can. Then he dipped in his penis. It hurt the first time, but after that not so much, and then not at all. He kept dipping and dipping. It got back to the normal size, and he should have been pleased with that. But Potchikoo got grandiose ideas.

He kept dipping and dipping. He melted more wax, more and more, and kept dipping, until he was so large he could hardly stagger out the door. Luckily, the wheelbarrow was sitting in the path. He grabbed the handles and wheeled it before him into town.

There was only one road in the village then. Potchikoo went there with his wheelbarrow, calling for women. He crossed the village twice. Mothers came out in wonder, saw what was in the wheelbarrow, and whisked their daughters inside. Everybody was disgusted and scolding and indignant, except for one woman. She lived at the end of the road. Her door was always open, and she was large.

Even now, we can't use her name, this Mrs. B. No man satisfied her. But that day, Potchikoo wheeled his barrow in, and then, for once, her door was shut.

Potchikoo and Mrs. B went rolling through the house. The walls shuddered, and people standing around outside thought the whole place might collapse. Potchikoo was shaken from side to side, powerfully, as if he were on a ride at the carnival. But eventually, of course, the heat of their union softened and wilted Potchikoo back to nothing. Mrs. B was disgusted and threw him out back, into the weeds. From there he crept home to Josette, and on the crooked path he took to avoid others, he tried to think of new ways he might please her.

Potchikoo's Mean Twin

To his relief, nature returned manhood to Potchikoo in several weeks. But his troubles weren't over. One day, the police appeared. They said Potchikoo had been seen stealing fence posts down the road. But they found no stolen fence posts on his property, so they did not arrest him.

More accusations were heard.

Potchikoo threw rocks at a nun, howled like a dog, and barked until she chased him off. He got drunk and tossed a pool cue out the window of the Stumble Inn. The pool cue hit the tribal chairman on the shoulder and caused a bruise. Potchikoo ran down the street laughing, flung off his clothes, ran naked through the trading store. He ripped antennas from twenty cars. He broke a portable radio that belonged to a widow, her only comfort. If a friendly dog came up to this bad Potchikoo, he lashed out with his foot. He screamed at children until tears came into their eyes, and then he knocked down the one road sign the government had seen fit to place on the reservation.

The sign was red, planted in the very middle of town, and said STOP. People were naturally proud of the sign. So there was finally a decision to lock Potchikoo in jail. When the police came to get him, he went quite willingly because he was so confused.

But here's what happened.

While Potchikoo was locked up, under the eyes of the tribal sheriff, his mean twin went out and caused some mischief near the school by starting a grass fire. So now the people knew the trouble wasn't caused by Old Man Potchikoo. And next time the bad twin was seen, Josette followed him. He ran very fast, until he reached the chain link fence around the graveyard. Josette saw him jump over the fence and dodge among the stones. Then the twin got to the place where Potchikoo had been buried, lifted the ground like a lid, and wiggled under.

How Josette Takes Care of It

So the trouble was that Potchikoo had left his old body in the ground, empty, and something bad had found a place to live.

The people said the only thing to do was trap the mean twin and then get rid of him. But no one could agree on how to do it. People just talked and planned, no one acted. Finally Josette had to take the matter into her own hands.

One day she made a big pot of stew, and into it she put a bird. Into the roasted bird, Josette put a bit of blue plaster that had fallen off the Blessed Virgin's robe while she cleaned the altar. She took the stew and left the whole pot just outside the cemetery fence. From her hiding place deep in a lilac bush, she saw the mean twin creep forth. He took the pot in his hands and gulped down every morsel, then munched the bird up, bones and all. Stuffed full, he lay down to sleep. He snored. After a while, he woke and looked around himself, very quietly. That was when Josette came out of the bush.

"In the name of the Holy Mother of God!" she cried. "Depart!"

So the thing stepped out of Potchikoo's old body, all hairless and smooth and wet and gray. But Josette had no pity. She pointed sternly at the dark stand of pines, where no one went, and slowly, with many a sigh and backward look, the thing walked over there.

Potchikoo's old body lay, crumpled like a worn suit of clothes, where the thing had stepped out. Right there, Josette made a fire, a little fire. When the blaze was very hot, she threw in the empty skin. It crackled in the flames, shed sparks, and was finally reduced to a crisp of ashes, which Josette brushed carefully into a little sack, and saved in her purse.

PART FIVE ∿

The Fence 〜〜

Then one day the gray rags vanish
and the sweet wind rattles her sash.
Her secrets bloom hot. I'm wild for everything.
My body is a golden armor around my unborn child's body,
and I'll die happy, here on the ground.
I bend to the mixture of dirt, chopped hay,
grindings of coffee from our dark winter breakfasts.
I spoon the rich substance around the acid-loving shrubs.
I tear down last year's drunken vines,
pull the black rug off the bed of asparagus
and lie there, knowing by June I'll push the baby out
as easily as seed wings fold back from the cotyledon.
I see the first leaf already, the veined tongue
rigid between the thighs of the runner beans.
I know how the shoot will complicate itself
as roots fill the trench.
Here is the link fence, the stem doubling toward it,
and something I've never witnessed.
One moment the young plant trembles on its stalk.
The next, it has already gripped the wire.
Now it will continue to climb, dragging rude blossoms
to the other side
until in summer fruit like green scimitars,
the frieze of vines, and then the small body
spread before me in need
drinking light from the shifting wall of my body,
and the fingers, tiny stems wavering to mine,
flexing for the ascent.

Ninth Month ~~

This is the last month, the petrified forest
and the lake which has long since turned to grass.
The sun roars over, casting its light and absence
in identical seams. One day. Another.
The child sleeps on in its capsized boat.

The hull is weathered silver and our sleep is green and dark.
Dreams of the rower, hands curled in the shape of oars
listening for the cries of the alabaster birds. But all
is silent, the animals hurled into quartz.
Our bed is the wrecked blue island of time and love.

Black steeples, black shavings of magnetized iron,
through which the moon parades her wastes,
drawing the fruit from the female body,
pulling water like blankets up other shores.

Then slowly the sky is colored in, the snow
falls evenly into the blackness of cisterns.
The steel wings fan open that will part us from each other
and the waves break and fall according to their discipline.

Breath that moves on the waters.
Small boat, small rower.

Birth ~~

When they were wild
When they were not yet human
When they could have been anything,
I was on the other side ready with milk to lure them,
And their father, too, each name a net in his hands.

S u n f l o w e r s ～✦～

When I walk into their bedroom at night
their cries fill my own mouth
so full of accurate misery,
heat flush, a stabbing in the gums,
something blind, with many hooks.
I drag the older one up into my arms
and talk until she opens her eyes.
The other
with her punishing beauty
ferments in a ball, soaked,
hot and vinegary.
I wash her.
The rag is sour.
But the talcum I shake into my palm
is dry and sweet.
Slowly, with both my hands,
I smooth along the hairline, throbbing with attention,
across the wishbone, the heart
vivid as a light,
down the arms, their tiny velvet muscles,
the arching torso, missing only the cleft
inside the diaper,
then the fat thighs, wet backs of the knees,
and the feet, small wooden apples.
Now their father brings the cold milk in bottles.
The doors shut.
We plunge into a dense sleep
that opens to a field of sunflowers,

each one of them a glowing clock,
turned, soft and bristling, to the bronze
face of the old god
who floats over us and burns.

Translucence ~~~

The water table's dropping in the heat,
and all the cats are out,
scrawny, pregnant, screaming in the rafters
of the red garage. I'm down
with something mild and local, viral,
undistinguished as house wine
but strange, nevertheless,
enough to outline chairs with smoky light.

Your face, kind, mildly anxious, bored,
sweeps in from the other brisk old world.
You check my forehead, bid
me breathe onto your hand, and nod.

It's not until you've gone to sleep downstairs
and all the children turning in their beds
turn dim and weedy, husked with leaves and soot,
not mine at all, as if the woods had tossed them
carapaced in mud, into our house, brown copice
sprouting in their hair, it's not until

the aspirin's hollow in my ear like bees,
a drumming roar that bounces off the walls,
and shakes me from the bed onto the floor,
I call your name and wrap in rippling stars
as everything's come back. The cats outdoors
claw themselves together in a knot.

I'm nothing like you, nothing, suddenly,
although your voice comes large as dusk now, calm,
and brims around me like a well,
and black flowers in the black grass bloom.

It was like this when I had the baby.
Looking at you in extremity,
so trapped in flesh, the body's gates
slammed closed between us.
And the spirit in the sinking light,
holding its own sharp elbows.

The Glass and the Bowl ~~~

The father pours the milk from his glass
into the cup of the child,
and as the child drinks
the whiteness, opening
her throat to the good taste
eagerly, the father is filled.
He closes the refrigerator
on its light, he walks out
under the bowl of frozen darkness
and nothing seems withheld from him.
Overhead, the burst ropes of stars,
the buckets of craters,
the chaos of heaven, absence
of refuge in the design.
Yet down here, his daughter
in her quilts, under patterns
of diamonds and novas,
full of rich milk,
sleeping.

Wild Plums ～

The son must come of age
in the margins and hem
of his mother's cloak.
It is spread over three dark meadows
where the wind dies.
Hard for him to enter these places.
In one, her voice is a pastel material,
peach and weightless as catalogue silks.
Crushed helmets are in another field,
dull red and pocked.
The things she can rust with her tears!
And the tin swords that wilt
and the vines that carelessly
pull down towers.
These things do her bidding even while she sleeps!
It is better for him to go to that last place,
where chairs are set, a table loaded
with food gathered out of the earth.
The roots of cattail, daylilies,
the dandelion's sawtooth leaves,
the bitterness boiled from the unopened flowers
of the milkweed.
Even she cannot claim to have provided all of this.
He eats everything in front of him.
There is never enough.
Fistfuls and mouthfuls of the wild red plums.

The Flight 〜〆〜

He's sleeping but he's everywhere at once,
my son, my own tornado watch.

The sky lowering, the sky a hot cone
as the graves open and the living
leap down with bread and lanterns.

The boy whose fever I breathed in, whose palms
bore crooked lines, the callous thick, the frost
in his hair when we found him sleeping
in the shattered pine.

                    Sheet lightning
trembled in the west and at the Drive-in
word came on the crackling microphone.

Too late, the weather was upon us, whistling
and groaning like the engine of a train.

We ripped the speakers out by the roots and drove
east, east in the slashing rain.

The Return ~~

The scarred trees twisted and the locked garage
held all my secrets, and my father's hunting bows
unstrung, my mother's empty canning bottles.
Once a mouse slipped in and tipped the glass
straight up so that it starved dead
at the bottom of a clear well.
I found a husk, a smear of grease, and a calm
odor of the ancient.

All winter, I dug tunnels in the snow
that mounted, mounted to the eaves and blew
like dry foam off the ridgepole. In my den
the air was warm and supernatural.
The quiet hung around me like a bell
and I could hear my own heart jump
like a frog in my chest. The crushing weight

of church was up above. I hid and waited
while God crossed over like the Hindenberg
and roared, like my grandfather to his men
and traced the ground with his binocular vision
but never saw me, as I was blue
as the shadow in a chunk of snow,
as a glass horse in a glass stall.

Down here my breath iced the walls.
The snow fell deeper than I could crawl.
I was sealed back into the zero
and then at last the world went dark.

My body hummed itself to sleep
and her heart was my heart,
filling the close air,
slowing in the empty jar.

The Flood ~✶~

I was twelve the year I slept in the earth,
in a perfect room lined with scentless wood.
It was the best place, the basement.
In the rhythm of appliances,
a child sleeps as though she wasn't born.
The washer boomed into the night
like an emotional heart, the refrigerator knocked,
dragged out the bones and argued.
The furnace was a fiery lung, but I was safe,
surrounded by plumbing.

Over me, when everything had fallen into ruin,
I heard my parents rearrange the day's wreckage
into the shape of a bed.
I heard my sisters dig forward with their paws
and wedge themselves under its boards.
And then the snow came down, collapsing the sky
around us in a blank formation.

In the spring it happened, as it was meant to.
The violent rain surged through the walls,
forced me out the cellar hatch in a round blue tub.
The calls of my brothers came over the string-can telephone.
Come in! Do you read me! But I was gone.
The river hammered and bubbled through the drains,
the line snapped, their voices grew fierce as mosquitoes
dancing on the head of a pin, clouding the wreckage
I passed, as the flood rushed me over its wide surface,
shredding my nightgown, my shawl of stingers.

I left a white foam in my wake, a net
drifting underwater for the feet of my sisters and brothers.
And now I fear for them
stepping in the holes of it and pulled underneath
the current of my luck. Understand:
it was as if I could escape only by abandoning everything.
I didn't think of all that's left in the aftermath,
twisted in the slogged roots, the earth walls undermined, the wires
slipping from the poles, alive and dangerous, into the water.

Owls ~~~

The barred owls scream in the black pines,
searching for mates. Each night
the noise wakes me, a death
rattle, everything in sex that wounds.
There is nothing in the sound but raw need
of one feathered body for another.
Yet, even when they find one another,
there is no peace.

In Ojibwa, the owl is Kokoko, and not
even the smallest child loves the gentle sound
of the word. Because the hairball
of bones and vole teeth can be hidden
under snow, to kill the man who walks over it.
Because the owl looks behind itself to see you coming,
the vane of the feather does not disturb
air, and the barb is ominously soft.

Have you ever seen, at dusk,
an owl take flight from the throat of a dead tree?
Mist, troubled spirit.
You will notice only after
its great silver body has turned to bark.
The flight was soundless.

That is how we make love,
when there are people in the halls around us,
clashing dishes, filling their mouths
with air, with debris, pulling

switches and filters as the whole machinery
of life goes on, eliminating and eliminating
until there are just the two bodies
fiercely attached, the feathers
floating down and cleaving to their shapes.

The Ritual ～♪～

This house is old. For two hundred years
a woman has risen in the iron cold
of the deepest hour. She has arranged her body
with the child inside
to guard her sleeping husband with its light.
And that is why, so that we pass safely under God's heels
I leave my body beside you,
and ease myself out of our bed.

Downstairs, on the smooth table in the moon's spill,
all our meals are spread, the times
when someone had to leave,
when someone chewed the handle off the spoon,
when grease spattered and burned through my face as tears,
when the two, a boy and girl, loved each other so much
they fused at the joints and stared
in loss when they turned thirteen.
They clutched each other's knees in shock
when the right song on the radio,
when the hot sauce,
when the strange word was uttered.

The crack in the table widened. The new leaf
had to be stripped with acids and restored.
Now the floors are waxed and the wood gives off
its old finite gleam; the window sockets
glitter in the cold and the range
is clamped like a mouth on warm ashes.

Soon, I say to the unborn one turning
beneath the heart of the sleeping woman,
you will break from me and be recognized.
You will drink from me as the dark rushes by
then curl with your ear to your father's chest
all night, the first night,
calmed by his heart instead of mine in your new life.

In the hour of the wolf, the hour of the horn,
the claw, the lead pipe, and the oiled barrel of roulette,
the woman walks into the room
of her small son or daughter
whose upper lip is flaked with dry milk
who sleeps with arms flung wide
in furious green flight. She whispers
every living word she knows:
I bind the net beneath you with the tendons of my wrist.
I call the guardian owl
who terrifies harm. I hold the sheaf
of lucky flowers to your forehead.

When the black bolt slides in the lock
and the windows are flocked with ferns of crystal,
I return to our bed and climb down the wedding quilt,
the twelve-branched tree of life.
When we sleep together, when we breathe each other's breath,
the crown spreads, the leaves scorch to bronze,
the slow growth accelerates
and the trunk swells, ring upon ring,
until the slightest twigs scrape at the solid frost-blue
of the floor of heaven.
In the tremor of the long, receding footsteps
we awaken. The day is ordinary,
sunlight fans across the ceiling.